Dave,

May God pour out his richest blessings upon you.

Congratulations

Joni
6-5-83

Handbook of Help and Hope

Promises and Guidance from the Bible

BOB COCHRAN

Tyndale House Publishers, Inc.   Wheaton, Illinois

Most of the Bible verses quoted directly are from *The Living Bible* and are used by permission. Other topical statements are adapted from several versions of the Bible.

Library of Congress Catalog Card Number 80-53683. ISBN 0-8423-1279-X, paper. Copyright © 1980 by Bob Cochran. All rights reserved. First printing, March 1981. Printed in the United States of America.

To

BOB KRULISH

DOUG BURLEIGH

and the

YOUNG LIFE LEADERS

of the

PACIFIC NORTHWEST

CONTENTS

INTRODUCTION 9

SECTION I TOPICAL INDEX
ABORTION 15
ADULTERY 16
ALCOHOL 16
ANGER 17
ANXIETY 17
ARGUE 19
ASSOCIATIONS 19
AUTHORITY 20
BIBLE (See Scripture)
BITTERNESS 20
BODY 21
CALAMITY 21
CHANGE (See Conversion)
CHURCH 23
COMMANDMENT 23
CONDUCT 24
CONFESSION 26
CONSCIENCE 26
CONVERSION 27
CONVICTION 29
COUNSELING 29
COVETOUSNESS (See Desire)
DATING (See Friendship)
DEATH 30
DEBT (See Finance)
DECISION-MAKING 31
DEPRESSION (from guilt) 31
DEPRESSION (from rejection) 32
DESIRE 33
DESPAIR (See Depression; Encouragement) 34
DISCIPLES 35
DISCIPLINE 35
DIVORCE 36
DOUBT 37
DRUGS 37
DRUNKENNESS 38
ENCOURAGEMENT 38
ENVY 40
FAMILY RELATIONSHIPS 41
FEAR 43
FINANCES 44
FORGIVENESS 45
FORNICATION 47
FREEDOM 48
FRIENDSHIP 48
FRUIT OF THE SPIRIT 49
GIFTS OF THE SPIRIT 49
GLUTTONY 50
GOSSIP 50
GRIEF 50

GUIDANCE 51
GUILT (See Depression)
HABIT 52
HARDNESS (See Love; Pride)
HATRED 53
HOLINESS 53
HOMOSEXUALITY 55
HOPE 55
HUMILITY 56
INSECURITY (See Security)
JEALOUSY 57
JUDGING (by man) 58
JUDGMENT (of man) 59
LAZINESS 60
LONELINESS 60
LOVE 61
LUST (See Desire)
LYING 63
NARCOTICS (See Drugs)
NERVOUSNESS (See Fear)
OBEDIENCE 64
OCCULT 65
PEACE 66
PRAYER 67
PRIDE 68
PURITY (See Holiness)
REBELLION (See Obedience)
RECONCILIATION 69
REJECTION (See Depression)
REPENTANCE 69
REPROVE 70
RESENTMENT 72
REVENGE (See Forgiveness)
SALVATION (need) 72
SALVATION (means) 74
SCRIPTURE 76
SECURITY 78
SELF-WILL (See Authority)
SEX/SEXUALITY 78
SHAME 79
SIN 79
STEALING 80
SUICIDE (See Encouragement)
TALK 81
TEMPTATION/TRIALS 82
THINKING/THOUGHTS 83
UNFORGIVENESS (See Forgiveness)
WORK 84
WORRY 85

SECTION II COUNSELING AIDS
ATTITUDE DEVELOPMENT CHART 89
COUNSELING CHECK LIST 92

INTRODUCTION

This topical index of the Holy Scriptures has been designed for the person who counsels others about personal problems. Its depth should satisfy the demands of clergy and professional counselors; its simplicity and annotated form should make it equally useful for group leaders, youth workers, and others who desire to use God's Word to minister to the problems of people.

Our Creator God did not make us and then leave us to fight our way through life alone. In the Bible he has given us all the knowledge we need in order to live in harmony with the rest of his creation. This doesn't mean, though, that the Bible is a book of rules which can be followed to achieve happiness. God wants us to have a relationship with him, not with a book. Happiness can be found only through the Lordship of Christ Jesus. Fulfillment comes only through him and dynamic guidance comes only through *the* Counselor, the Holy Spirit of God.

Knowledge of the living Word, Jesus, comes to us from the written Word, the Bible. But more than that: In his written Word, a benevolent God has given us principles which, if lived out, will put us in harmony with his will, which will in turn lead to a harmonious life. In his Word we learn the character of God and we learn how to live to please him.

Most of all, we believe that the Counselor, the Holy Spirit, uses as his first and most important means of counseling the written Word which he inspired.

The Scripture passages listed under each heading are not intended as a panacea for the problem in the heading. They should not be used as "proof texts," nor should they be held as clubs over a counselee's head. They are intended as *entries,* starting points to begin meditating on God's Word. The context and intent of the passage, as well as the meaning of the passage itself, are important to understand and convey to the counselee.

Instead of this index being merely a list of chapter and verse references, each reference includes some description of what will be found there. Sometimes the verse or passage itself is given. When this is done the author has used the text from *The Living Bible* as being most readily adaptable to counseling situations. Often, however, words and phrases and paraphrases are used in such a way as to enhance the use of this index as a reference index. Too few words would not convey enough meaning; too many would make it cumbersome. Sometimes the description given is but a note which the author has found meaningful and helpful in using this in his own ministry.

In most cases, the Scripture references are listed in their biblical sequence under each heading to aid in finding them. When they are not, it is because presentation to the counselee in the sequence given would be of benefit.

Where it would be helpful, either because a particular Scripture passage strongly identified with the heading or because some nonbiblical information would be useful, an introductory paragraph follows the heading title.

One feature of this index is the ample space that is provided following each heading for the insertion of a counselor's own references.

The first step in the use of this index should be to thoroughly familiarize oneself with the Contents. Learn how the index is structured and how to relate *your* thought patterns to *it*. Next, get familiar with the listed Scriptures, especially for those topics which most frequently occur in your ministry. Since these references are merely *entries*, you will want to study the whole passage in which it occurs and, with the aid of a cross-referenced Bible, look up the related passages.

To make this index more useful to those who counsel only occasionally, there is a second section containing two counseling aids intended primarily to help those who have not had professional training in counseling, yet who find themselves in a position of having to counsel.

11

SECTION 1
Topical Index

ABORTION

A human fetus, from the moment he or she is conceived, is a growing, living, human being. One common method of aborting this infant is to inject a strong salt solution into the womb. This burns the fetus to death and he is then aborted black, just as if he had been burned in a fire. (See below, Leviticus 20:2, 3.) Regardless of the method used, the principle is the same: abortion is the murder of a child.

The sixth commandment is, "You must not murder." (Cf. Matthew 19:18) Exodus 20:13

The penalty for murder is death because, "to kill a man is to kill one made like God." Genesis 9:5, 6

God forbids anyone to "sacrifice his child as a burnt offering." Leviticus 20:2, 3

God calls it an "incredible evil." Jeremiah 32:35

The penalty for it is the same as for any murder. Deuteronomy 18:10

The Lord God forms human beings in the womb. (Cf. Job 31:15; Isaiah 44:2, 24) Psalm 139:13

John the Baptist leaped in the womb. Luke 1:41, 44

ADULTERY
See also, Fornication

The term *adultery* refers to illicit sexual intercourse between a person and the spouse of another.

The seventh commandment is, "You must not commit adultery." Exodus 20:14

"The man who commits adultery...destroys his own soul." Proverbs 6:32

The prayers of an unfaithful husband are not answered. Malachi 2:13-16

Anyone who even looks at a woman lustfully has committed adultery. Matthew 5:28

"From the heart come evil thoughts...adultery." Matthew 15:19

Adulterers will have no share in God's Kingdom. 1 Corinthians 6:9

Don't commit adultery; God will punish those who do. Hebrews 13:4

ALCOHOL
See also, Drunkenness

God has given man wine to make him glad. Psalm 104:15

Jesus turns water into wine at a party. John 2:6-10

One should not drink alcohol if doing it offends someone or causes him to sin. Romans 14:21

A little wine is good for the stomach. 1 Timothy 5:23

ANGER

"A short-tempered man is a fool." Proverbs 14:17

"A wise man controls his temper. He knows that anger causes mistakes." Proverbs 14:29

"A quick-tempered man starts fights; a cool-tempered man tries to stop them." Proverbs 15:18

"A wise man restrains his anger and overlooks insults." Proverbs 19:11

"Keep away from angry, short-tempered men." Proverbs 22:24

A man without self-control is defenseless. Proverbs 25:28

"A wise man holds his temper in and cools it." Proverbs 29:11

"A hot-tempered man...gets into all kinds of trouble." Proverbs 29:22

"If you are angry, don't sin...Don't let the sun go down with you still angry." Ephesians 4:26

One should be slow to get angry; anger does not promote righteousness. James 1:19, 20

ANXIETY
See also, Hope, Security, Worry

"The eternal God is your Refuge." Deuteronomy 33:27

Though he slay me, yet will I hope in God.... Job 13:15

"Never envy the wicked. Soon they...disappear. Trust in the Lord instead." Psalm 37:1-3

"Trust in God...He will make you smile again." Psalm 43:5

"God is our refuge and strength...so we need not fear even if the world blows up." Psalm 46:1, 2

Whom have we in heaven but God?...Though our health fails and spirits droop, still God remains. Psalm 73:25, 26

"No good thing will God withhold from those who walk along his paths." Psalm 84:11

God never grows faint or weary; those that wait upon him shall renew their strength. Isaiah 40:28-31

Fear not, for God is with you; he will strengthen, help, and uphold you. Isaiah 41:10

When you go through great trouble and oppression, God will be with you. Isaiah 43:2

Don't worry about things and do not be anxious about tomorrow. Matthew 6:25-34

Jesus said to come to him and he would give you rest. Matthew 11:28-30

"All that happens to us is working for our good if we love God." Romans 8:28

"God has said, 'I will never, *never* fail you nor forsake you.'...I am not afraid of anything that mere man can do to me." Hebrews 13:5, 6

Give your worries to God because he cares for you. 1 Peter 5:7

ARGUE
See also, Anger

"A soft answer turns away wrath." Proverbs 15:1

"Only fools insist on quarreling." Proverbs 20:3

ASSOCIATIONS

"Oh, the joys of those who do not follow evil men's advice, who do not hang around with sinners.... All they do shall prosper." Psalm 1

"Can a man hold fire against his chest and not be burned?" Proverbs 6:27

"Be with wise men and become wise. Be with evil men and become evil." Proverbs 13:20

"Keep away from angry, short-tempered men." Proverbs 22:24, 25

Don't be with heavy drinkers of wine or with gluttonous eaters. Proverbs 23:20

"Don't visit your neighbor too often, or you will outwear your welcome." Proverbs 25:17

Don't associate with a pretended Christian who is immoral, greedy, abusive, etc. 1 Corinthians 5:9-11

Do not have close relationships (i.e., engagement, business, etc.) with unbelievers; no partnership, no fellowship, nothing in common.
2 Corinthians 6:14, 15

Come out and be separate. (Cf. Revelation 18:4)
2 Corinthians 6:17

Flee the lusts of youth; pursue integrity with Christian brothers. 2 Timothy 2:22

AUTHORITY

"Obey the government, for God is the one who has put it there. There is no government anywhere that God has not placed in power. So those who refuse to obey the laws of the land are refusing to obey God, and punishment will follow." Romans 13:1, 2

"It is good for a young man to be under discipline." Lamentations 3:27

When human authority conflicts with God's Word, one should obey God rather than men. (Cf. Acts 4:19, 20) Acts 5:29

The headship principle. 1 Corinthians 11:3-12

"Obey every law of your government." (But see above, Acts 5:29.) 1 Peter 2:13

BIBLE
(See Scripture)

BITTERNESS
See also, Forgiveness, Resentment

When my heart was grieved and embittered, I was senseless and ignorant, a brute beast before you. Psalm 73:21, 22

No one in the world is righteous...whose mouth is full of cursing and bitterness. Romans 3:10-14

Get rid of all bitterness. Ephesians 4:31

"Watch out that no bitterness takes root among you." Hebrews 12:15

BODY

"Give your bodies to God...a living sacrifice." Romans 12:1

You (plural) are God's temple....If anyone defiles it, God will destroy him. 1 Corinthians 3:16, 17

Don't engage in sexual immorality, a sin against one's own body. 1 Corinthians 6:18-20

Heavenly bodies and earthly bodies.
1 Corinthians 15:35-49

CALAMITY

Do afflictions, calamities, and disasters all come upon us by chance? Are they just coincidence? Are we plagued by the devil? Do we really get into "accidents"? Do "misfortunes" really happen to us? *Why* do they happen? In 1 Samuel 6, the Philistines wanted to know if their troubles had come by chance or were sent from God. The answer (from God) is in verse 12; compare it with verse 9.

"We toss the coin, but it is the Lord who controls its decision." ("Luck" is not biblical.) Proverbs 16:33

Jesus prayed that Christians be kept, "safe from Satan's power." John 17:15

The devil cannot touch Christians. 1 John 5:18

The devil may be used to do God's will.
(Cf. Genesis 50:20; 1 Samuel 16:14 ff.;
Job 1:8, 12, 13; 2:3, 6; 2 Corinthians 12:7)
2 Timothy 2:26

Jesus alone is God, who sends good times and bad.
(Cf. Deuteronomy 32:39; Lamentations 3:38)
Isaiah 45:6, 7

God may cause/create calamity and disaster.
(Cf. Jeremiah 4:6) Amos 3:6

...Bones which God has broken. Psalm 51:8

"The Lord has called down a famine...."
2 Kings 8:1

"And I [God] will send massacre and famine and disease...." (Cf. Jeremiah 27:8; 29:17, 18)
Jeremiah 24:10

"I [God] have wounded you cruelly...because your guilt is great." Jeremiah 30:14, 15

"Although God gives him grief, yet he will show compassion too....For he does not enjoy afflicting men and causing sorrow." Lamentations 3:32, 33

CHANGE
(See Conversion)

CHURCH

Bring all that God commands and rejoice before him—not to just any place but only to where God shall choose. Deuteronomy 12:8-14

Where two or three gather together because they are his, Jesus will be there among them. Matthew 18:20

"Those who preach the gospel should be supported by those who accept it." 1 Corinthians 9:14

The meaning of Communion. 1 Corinthians 10:16, 17

The Communion Service. 1 Corinthians 11:23-29

"Those who are taught the Word of God should help their teachers by paying them." Galatians 6:6

"The church of the living God...contains and holds high the truth of God." 1 Timothy 3:15

"Pastors who do their work well should be paid well and should be highly appreciated. Those who work deserve their pay." 1 Timothy 5:17, 18

"Let us not neglect our church meetings."
Hebrews 10:25

COMMANDMENT

The Ten Commandments. Exodus 20:3-17

A new commandment: Love one another. John 13:34

The true love of God is obeying his commandments.
1 John 5:3

CONDUCT
See also, Holiness and Sex/Sexuality

"[God] has told you what he wants, and this is all it is: to be fair and just and merciful, and to walk humbly with your God." Micah 6:8

"A woman must not wear men's clothing, and a man must not wear women's clothing." Deuteronomy 22:5

God gets no pleasure from wickedness: boasting, lying, murder, deceiving. Psalm 5:4-6

"Ask where the good road is, the godly paths you used to walk in, in the days of long ago. Travel there...." Jeremiah 6:16

"Don't copy the behavior and customs of this world, but be a new and different person with a fresh newness in all you do and think." Romans 12:2

"Please the other fellow, not ourselves, and do what is for his good." Romans 15:1, 2

Be wise in what is good and innocent in what is evil. Romans 16:19

Adulterers, homosexuals, thieves, greedy people, drunkards, slanderers, and robbers will have no share in God's kingdom. 1 Corinthians 6:9, 10

Be careful that your Christian liberty doesn't cause someone with a weak conscience to sin. 1 Corinthians 8:9-13

Don't seek your own advantage but your neighbor's. 1 Corinthians 10:24

Some things are all right to do if done innocently but not if brought to one's attention.
1 Corinthians 10:27-29

Do everything to the glory of God.
1 Corinthians 10:31

Bear one another's burdens but carry your own load.
Galatians 6:2, 5

God is not mocked; one reaps what he sows.
Galatians 6:7, 8

Always be kind, especially to Christians. Galatians 6:10

Immorality and impurity should not even be mentioned; nor should there be foul talk or coarse jokes.
Ephesians 5:3, 4

Your ambition should be "to live a quiet life, minding your own business and doing your own work."
1 Thessalonians 4:11

Show brotherly love and hospitality. Hebrews 13:1, 2

"Stay away from the love of money; be satisfied with what you have." Hebrews 13:5

Take care of orphans and widows. James 1:27

"Faith that doesn't show itself by good works is no faith at all—it is dead and useless." James 2:14-18

Behave well and so silence the ignorance of foolish men. 1 Peter 2:15

"Show respect for everyone. Love Christians everywhere. Fear God and honor the government."
1 Peter 2:17

"When a person has escaped from the wicked ways of the world by learning about our Lord and Savior Jesus Christ, and then gets tangled up with sin and becomes its slave again, he is worse off than he was before."
2 Peter 2:20, 21

CONFESSION

"When I wouldn't admit what a sinner I was, my dishonesty made me miserable." Psalm 32:3, 4

"A man who refuses to admit his mistakes can never be successful. But if he confesses and forsakes them, he gets another chance." Proverbs 28:13

Confess your faults to one another. James 5:16

"If we confess our sins to [God], he can be depended on to forgive us and to cleanse us from every wrong." 1 John 1:9

CONSCIENCE

"All day and all night your hand was heavy on me. My strength evaporated like water on a sunny day."
Psalm 32:4

"There is no peace for the wicked." Isaiah 48:22

The heart is deceitful but God searches the heart.
Jeremiah 17:9, 10

"Always maintain a clear conscience." Acts 24:16

Your conscience bears witness that the Law is written in your heart. Romans 2:15

What we do is wrong if it causes others to stumble. (Cf. 1 Corinthians 8:9, 12) Romans 14:15, 20, 21

Having a clear conscience does not make one innocent. 1 Corinthians 4:4

Some things are all right to do if done innocently but would be a sin if brought to one's attention. 1 Corinthians 10:27-29

"Always keep your conscience clear, doing what you know is right." 1 Timothy 1:19

Maintain a clear conscience so that a slanderer may be put to shame. 1 Peter 3:16

CONVERSION

"When someone becomes a Christian he becomes a brand new person inside. He is not the same any more. A new life has begun!" 2 Corinthians 5:17

"Put [your sins] behind you and receive a new heart and a new spirit." Ezekiel 18:31

"I will give you a new heart...and put my Spirit within you." Ezekiel 36:25-27

"Don't copy the behavior and customs of this world, but be a new and different person with a fresh newness in all you do and think." Romans 12:2

"Live no longer as the unsaved do." Ephesians 4:17

"Throw off your old evil nature." Ephesians 4:22

"Your attitudes and thoughts must all be constantly changing for the better." Ephesians 4:23

"Clothe yourself with this [holy and good] new nature." Ephesians 4:24

"Stop lying to each other; tell the truth." Ephesians 4:25

A thief must stop stealing and begin to work. Ephesians 4:28

"Don't use bad language. Say only what is good and helpful." Ephesians 4:29

Instead of being mean and bad-tempered, be kind, tenderhearted, and forgiving. Ephesians 4:31, 32

Be thankful instead of using foul language and telling coarse jokes. Ephesians 5:4

"Don't act thoughtlessly, but try to find out and do whatever the Lord wants you to." Ephesians 5:17

"Let heaven fill your thoughts; don't spend your time worrying about things down here." Colossians 3:2

Lay aside the old self and put on the new self. Colossians 3:9, 10

Do not pay back evil for evil but do good. 1 Thessalonians 5:15

Don't neglect to meet together but encourage one another. Hebrews 10:25

Don't repay evil for evil but instead pray God's blessings on your enemies. 1 Peter 3:9

Don't imitate evil but good. 3 John 11

CONVICTION

The Holy Spirit will convict. John 16:8-11

COUNSELING
See also, Scripture

"Only the person involved can know his own bitterness or joy—no one else can really share it." Proverbs 14:10

I will teach your ways to others. Psalm 51:13

"A fool thinks he needs no advice, but a wise man listens to others." Proverbs 12:15

"There is safety in many counselors." (Cf. Proverbs 11:14) Proverbs 24:6

A definition of counseling: to give understanding, show the path of justice, and teach knowledge and discernment. Isaiah 40:14

The Holy Spirit will teach you and remind you of what Jesus said. John 14:26

The Holy Spirit will convict of sin, righteousness, and judgment. John 16:8

The Holy Spirit will guide you into all truth. John 16:13

Christians are able to counsel one another. (Cf. 2 Timothy 3:16, 17) Romans 15:14

The goal of counseling is love from a pure heart, a clear conscience, and strong faith. 1 Timothy 1:5

COVETOUSNESS
See Desire

DATING
See Friendship

DEATH

"Even when walking through the dark valley of death I will not be afraid...." Psalm 23:4

"[God's] loved ones are very precious to him and he does not lightly let them die." Psalm 116:15

"The godly have a refuge when they die." Proverbs 14:32

"Anyone who believes in me [Jesus], even though he dies like anyone else, shall live again. He is given eternal life...and shall never perish." John 11:25, 26

"Everyone dies.... But all who are related to Christ will rise again." 1 Corinthians 15:22

"We are not afraid, but are quite content to die, for then we will be at home with the Lord." (Cf. 2 Corinthians 5:1) 2 Corinthians 5:8

"To me, living means opportunities for Christ, and dying—well, that's better yet!" Philippians 1:21

It is better to depart and be with Christ. Phil. 1:23

"[Christ] died for us so that we can live with him forever." 1 Thessalonians 5:10

Jesus set free those in slavery to fear of death. Hebrews 2:14, 15

DEBT
See Finance

DECISION-MAKING
See also, Judging, Guidance

"We can make our plans, but the final outcome is in God's hands." Proverbs 16:1

"We toss the coin, but it is the Lord who controls its decision." Proverbs 16:33

"What a shame—yes, how stupid!—to decide before knowing the facts!" Proverbs 18:13

"It is dangerous and sinful to rush into the unknown." Proverbs 19:2

Deciding between Christians: accept mistreatment rather than a lawsuit. 1 Corinthians 6:4-8

Let the peace of Christ rule (arbitrate, or referee) in your hearts. Colossians 3:15, KJV

DEPRESSION (from guilt)
See also, Reconciliation, Repentance

"All day and all night your hand was heavy on me. My strength evaporated like water on a sunny day." (Cf. Job 23:2) Psalm 32:4

God's hand presses down on me. Psalm 38:2

"The wicked man is doomed by his own sins; they are ropes that catch and hold him." Proverbs 5:22

"Return to the Lord your God, for he is gracious and merciful. He is not easily angered; he is full of kindness, and anxious not to punish you." Joel 2:13

"[God] took away all our sins through the blood of his Son, by whom we are saved." Ephesians 1:7

"[God's Son] bought our freedom with his blood and forgave us all our sins." Colossians 1:13, 14

"If we confess our sins to [God], he can be depended on to forgive us and to cleanse us from every wrong." 1 John 1:9

DEPRESSION (from rejection)
See also, Encouragement, Temptation/Trials

"If my father and mother should abandon me, [God] would welcome and comfort me." Psalm 27:10

"O my soul, why be so gloomy and discouraged? Trust in God! I shall again praise him." Psalm 43:5

"Give your burdens to the Lord. He will carry them. He will not permit the godly to slip or fall."
Psalm 55:22

The consolation of God's protection. Psalm 121

When you go through trouble and oppression God will be with you. Isaiah 43:2

Although God may bring grief, he will show compassion. Lamentations 3:32, 33

Not one sparrow falls to the ground without God; he has counted every hair on every head.
(Cf. Luke 12:6, 7) Matthew 10:29-31

"We know that all that happens to us is working for our good if we love God." Romans 8:28

Christians are protected by the power of God. (Cf. Psalm 145:20) 1 Peter 1:5

"Let [God] have all your worries and cares, for he is always thinking about you and watching everything that concerns you." 1 Peter 5:7

The devil cannot harm Christians. 1 John 5:18

DESIRE

"All these wordly things, these evil desires—the craze for sex, the ambition to buy everything that appeals to you, and the pride that comes from wealth and importance—these are not from God. They are from this evil world itself. And this world is fading away, and these evil, forbidden things will go with it, but whoever keeps doing the will of God will live forever." 1 John 2:16, 17

The tenth commandment is, "You must not be envious...." Exodus 20:17

"Be delighted with the Lord. Then he will give you all your heart's desires." Psalm 37:4

"The Lord will not let a good man starve to death, nor will he let the wicked man's riches continue forever." Proverbs 10:3

"The wicked man's fears will all come true, and so will the good man's hopes." Proverbs 10:24

"Don't weary yourself trying to get rich. Why waste your time?" Proverbs 23:4

Where your treasure is, there is your heart.
Matthew 6:21

"Don't make plans to enjoy evil." Romans 13:14

Bring every thought into subjection to Christ.
2 Corinthians 10:5

Behave in a spiritual way and don't carry out the desires of the flesh. Galatians 5:16

We all once walked and indulged in fleshly desires.
Ephesians 2:3

"God is at work within you, helping you want to obey him, and then helpng you do what he wants."
Philippians 2:13

"The love of money is the first step toward all kinds of sin." 1 Timothy 6:9, 10

Turn from wordly passions and live self-controlled lives.
Titus 2:12

"Temptation is the pull of man's own evil thoughts and wishes." James 1:13-15

Don't conform to the evil desires you had when you lived in ignorance. 1 Peter 1:14

No longer live by human desires but for what God wants. 1 Peter 4:2, 3

DESPAIR
See Depression; Encouragement

DISCIPLES

Anyone wanting to follow Jesus must deny himself.
(Cf. Luke 14:33) Matthew 16:24

"If you merely obey [Jesus], you should not consider yourselves worthy of praise. For you have simply done your duty!" Luke 17:10

Disciples are recognized by their love for one another. John 13:35

"Follow my example, just as I follow Christ's."
1 Corinthians 11:1

DISCIPLINE
See also, Reprove

God will execute judgment because of failure to discipline. 1 Samuel 3:13

If you love your son you will discipline him.
Proverbs 13:24

"Punishment that hurts chases evil from the heart."
Proverbs 20:30

Train a child in the way he should go and when he is old he will not turn from it. Proverbs 22:6

"Discipline your son and he will give you happiness and peace of mind." Proverbs 29:15-19

"It is good for a young man to be under discipline."
Lamentations 3:27

The church should discipline a Christian if he sins.
(Cf. 1 Corinthians 5:11, 12) Matthew 18:15-20

Judgments from the Lord serve to discipline us.
1 Corinthians 11:32

"Children, obey your parents." Ephesians 6:1-3

Discipline (train) yourself for godliness. 1 Timothy 4:7

The Lord disciplines those whom he loves; Endure it for correction. (Cf. Proverbs 3:11, 12;
Revelation 3:19) Hebrews 12:5-11

DIVORCE

"From the very first [God] made man and woman to be joined together permanently in marriage; therefore a man is to leave his father and mother, and he and his wife are united so that they are no longer two, but one. And no man may separate what God has joined together." (Mark 10:6-9; Cf. Matthew 19:4-6)
Genesis 2:24

A man cannot remarry a woman he has divorced who has since remarried. Deuteronomy 24:1-4

God says he hates divorce. Malachi 2:16

"A man who divorces his wife except for fornication, causes her to commit adultery if she marries again. And he who marries her commits adultery."
Matthew 5:32

Divorce in the case of fornication. (Cf. Matthew 5:32)
Matthew 19:9

Divorce and remarriage. (Cf. Deuteronomy 24:1-4; Matthew 19:9; Luke 16:18) Mark 10:11, 12

Divorce regulations. 1 Corinthians 7:10-16

A widow is free to remarry without committing adultery. (Cf. Romans 7:2, 3) 1 Corinthians 7:39, 40

DOUBT

"The Lord has made everything for his own purposes—even the wicked." Proverbs 16:4

"All that's required is that you really believe and have no doubt." (Cf. Matthew 21:21) Mark 11:23-25

Ask in faith without doubting. James 1:6, 7

DRUGS

The word *sorcery (witchcraft)* in the New Testament is translated from the Greek word *pharmakia* (English, *pharmacy,* etc.) and signifies the nonmedicinal use of drugs. *Pharmakia* is also used in the Greek translation (LXX) of the cited Old Testament reference.

Disaster shall come upon those who persist in their drug use. Isaiah 47:9-12

The deeds of the flesh are...sorcery....Those who practice such things will not enter the kingdom of God. Galatians 5:19-21

Those who escaped the plagues did not repent of their sorcery. Revelation 9:20, 21

By sorcery were all the nations led astray.
Revelation 18:23

As for the...sorcerers...their lot is in the lake that burns with fire and sulphur. Revelation 21:8

Outside the gates (of the New Jerusalem) are...the sorcerers. Revelation 22:15

DRUNKENNESS
See also, Alcohol, Gluttony

Whoever gets drunk is a fool. Proverbs 20:1

Drunkards and gluttons are on their way to poverty.
Proverbs 23:21

"Whose heart is filled with anguish and sorrow? The one who spends long hours in the taverns."
Proverbs 23:29-35

Don't let Jesus' return find you carousing and drinking.
Luke 21:34

Do not get drunk with wine. Ephesians 5:18

ENCOURAGEMENT

"Be bold and strong! Banish fear and doubt! For remember, the Lord your God is with you wherever you go." (Cf. Deuteronomy 31:6, 8) Joshua 1:9

"The eyes of the Lord search back and forth across the whole earth, looking for people whose hearts are perfect toward him, so that he can show his great power in helping them." 2 Chronicles 16:9

"Don't be afraid!...The battle is not yours, but God's!"
2 Chronicles 20:15

"Jotham became powerful because he was careful to follow the path of the Lord his God."
2 Chronicles 27:6

"Do not despise the chastening of the Lord when you sin. For though he wounds, he binds and heals again. He will deliver you again and again, so that no evil can touch you." Job 5:17-20

"The good man does not escape all troubles—he has them too. But the Lord helps him in each and every one." Psalm 34:19

"The steps of good men are directed by the Lord. He delights in each step they take. If they fall it isn't fatal, for the Lord holds them with his hand."
Psalm 37:23, 24

"I have never seen the Lord forsake a man who loves him; nor have I seen the children of the godly go hungry." Psalm 37:25

"I shall again praise [God] for his wondrous help; he will make me smile again." Psalm 43:5

"God is a father to the fatherless; he gives justice to the widows." Psalm 68:5

"Commit your work to the Lord, then it will succeed."
Proverbs 16:3

"The Lord is wonderfully good to those who wait for him, to those who seek for him." (Cf. Isaiah 40:31; Psalm 27:14) Lamentations 3:25

"I [Jesus] have told you all this so that you will have peace of heart and mind. Here on earth you will have many trials and sorrows; but cheer up, for I have overcome the world." John 16:33

To the Christian (the called, according to God's purpose) who loves him, God works together all things for good. Romans 8:28

"Nothing will ever be able to separate us from the love of God demonstrated by our Lord Jesus Christ when he died for us." Romans 8:39

Do not lose heart; though our outer nature decays, our inner nature is renewed. Momentary light affliction produces eternal glory. 2 Corinthians 4:16, 17

"God has said, 'I will never, *never* fail you nor forsake you.' " Hebrews 13:5

"Let [God] have all your worries and cares, for he is always thinking about you and watching everything that concerns you." 1 Peter 5:7

ENVY
See also, Desire, Jealousy

"Don't be envious of evil men who prosper.... The wicked shall be destroyed." Psalm 37:7, 9

Regarding envy of the prosperity of the wicked. Psalm 73:2-20

"Don't envy evil men but continue to reverence the Lord." Proverbs 23:17

"Wherever there is jealousy or selfish ambition, there

will be disorder and every other kind of evil."
James 3:16

"Be done with dishonesty and jealousy and talking about others behind their backs." 1 Peter 2:1

FAMILY RELATIONSHIPS

"A man leaves his father and mother and is joined to his wife in such a way that the two become one person." Genesis 2:24

When God punishes people for their sins, the punishment continues upon the children, grandchildren, and great-grandchildren of those who hate him, but he lavishes his love upon thousands of those who love him and obey his commandments. Exodus 20:5, 6
but
If a son renounces his father's sinful behavior and walks in God's statutes, he shall not die for his father's sins. Ezekiel 18:14-17

"Children are a gift from God." Psalm 127:3

"How wonderful it is, how pleasant, when brothers live in harmony!" Psalm 133:1

"Only a fool despises his father's advice; a wise son considers each suggestion." Proverbs 15:5

"A dry crust eaten in peace is better than steak every day along with argument and strife." Proverbs 17:1

"An old man's grandchildren are his crowning glory. A child's glory is his father." Proverbs 17:6

"A rebellious son is a calamity to his father, and a nagging wife annoys like constant dripping."
Proverbs 19:13

"Discipline your son in his early years while there is hope. If you don't you will ruin his life."
Proverbs 19:18

"A son who mistreats his father or mother is a public disgrace." Proverbs 19:26

"It is better to live in a corner of an attic than in a beautiful home with a cranky, quarrelsome woman."
Proverbs 25:24

Be submissive to one another; Wives be subject to your husbands in every respect. (Cf. Genesis 12:10-20; 1 Corinthians 11:3-12);
Husbands, love your wives (Cf. Colossians 3:19)
Ephesians 5:21-33

Children, obey your parents. Fathers, don't frustrate and irritate your children. (Cf. Colossians 3:20, 21)
Ephesians 6:1-4

If a widow has children or grandchildren they should take care of her. 1 Timothy 5:4

"Anyone who won't care for his own relatives when they need help...is worse than the heathen."
1 Timothy 5:8

Older men are to be serious and unruffled. Older women are to be quiet and respectful. Young women...Young men. Titus 2:2-6

Wives be submissive to your husbands; husbands, be thoughtful of your wife's needs; everyone, be harmonious and sympathetic. 1 Peter 3:1-12

FEAR

"Because the Lord is my Shepherd, I have everything I need! He lets me rest in the meadow grass and leads me beside the quiet streams. He restores my failing health. He helps me do what honors him the most. Even when walking through the dark valley of death I will not be afraid, for you are close beside me, guarding, guiding all the way. You provide delicious food for me in the presence of my enemies. You have welcomed me as your guest; blessings overflow! Your goodness and unfailing kindness shall be with me all of my life, and afterwards I will live with you forever in your home." Psalm 23

"Don't be afraid, for the Lord will go before you and will be with you; he will not fail nor forsake you." Deuteronomy 31:6, 8

Seek the Lord and he will deliver you from all fear. Psalm 34:4

"The Lord is on my side, he will help me. Let those who hate me beware." (Cf. Psalm 27:1; Psalm 56:11) Psalm 118:7

"The wicked man's fears will all come true, and so will the good man's hopes." (Cf. Job 3:25) Proverbs 10:24

"Fear of men is a dangerous trap, but to trust in God means safety." Proverbs 29:25

"Don't be afraid of those who can kill only your bodies—but can't touch your souls!" Matthew 10:28-31

God has not given us a spirit of fear. 2 Timothy 1:7

Jesus set free those in fear of death. Hebrews 2:14, 15

Don't be terrified by threats; even if you suffer on account of righteousness, God will reward you for it.
1 Peter 3:13-17

Perfect love eliminates all fear. 1 John 4:18

FINANCES

"Trust the Lord completely; don't ever trust yourself. In everything you do, put God first, and he will direct you and crown your efforts with success. Proverbs 3:5, 6

"Don't worry about food—what to eat and drink; don't worry at all that God will provide it for you."
(Cf. Matthew 6:31) Luke 12:29

"He will always give you all you need from day to day if you will make the Kingdom of God your primary concern." (Cf. Matthew 6:33) Luke 12:31

"[God] will supply all your needs from his riches in glory." Philippians 4:19

"Be delighted with the Lord. Then he will give you all your heart's desires." Psalm 37:4, 5

"No good thing will [God] withhold from those who walk along his paths." Psalm 84:11

"He who does not work shall not eat."
2 Thessalonians 3:10

"If anyone is stealing he must stop it and begin using those hands of his for honest work so he can give to others in need." Ephesians 4:28

"The love of money is the first step toward all kinds of sin." 1 Timothy 6:10

"The earth belongs to God! Everything in all the world is his!" Psalm 24:1

Where to tithe? Where God shall choose for his name to dwell. Deuteronomy 12:11-14

Not tithing is robbing God. Malachi 3:8-11

Don't trust in money but use money to do good. 1 Timothy 6:17, 18

You don't have because you don't ask or because your goal is wrong: your own pleasures. James 4:2, 3

Owe nothing to anyone except love. Romans 13:8

"The borrower is servant to the lender." Proverbs 22:7

God is able to provide for us beyond our highest prayers, desires, thoughts, or hopes. Ephesians 3:20

"It is poor judgment to countersign another's note, to become responsible for his debts."
(Cf. Proverbs 6:1-5; 11:15; 22:26) Proverbs 17:18

Give freely. Luke 6:34, 35

FORGIVENESS (Cure for bitterness)
See also, Repentance

"God has removed our sins as far away from us as the east is from the west." Psalm 103:12

"Love forgets mistakes." Proverbs 17:9

"Don't repay evil for evil. Wait for the Lord to handle the matter." Proverbs 20:22

"Don't testify spitefully against an innocent neighbor...Don't say, 'Now I can pay him back for all his meanness to me.' " Proverbs 24:28, 29.

"Your heavenly Father will forgive you if you forgive those who sin against you; but if *you* refuse to forgive *them, he* will not forgive *you.*" Matthew 6:14, 15

"If a brother sins against you, go to him privately and confront him with his fault." Matthew 18:15

Jesus said we should forgive seventy times seven. Matthew 18:21, 22

"When you are praying, first forgive anyone you are holding a grudge against." Mark 11:25

"Rebuke your brother if he sins, and forgive him if he is sorry." Luke 17:3, 4

"Be kind to each other, tenderhearted, forgiving one another." Ephesians 4:32

"Be gentle and ready to forgive; never holding grudges. Remember, the Lord forgave you, so you must forgive others." Colossians 3:13

The prayer of faith will restore the sick and his sins will be forgiven. James 5:15

"If we confess our sins to [God], he can be depended on to forgive us and to cleanse us from every wrong." (See Luke 24:47: We must repent and turn to Jesus.) 1 John 1:9

FORNICATION
See also, Adultery, Sex/Sexuality

The term *fornication* refers to illicit sexual intercourse. In the Bible it may or may not include adultery, but usually does not, adultery being classed separately.

The lips of a loose woman may be as sweet as honey, but in the end, she is bitter. Proverbs 5:3-14

Stolen waters are sweet but the results are death and the depths of hell. Proverbs 9:13-18

From the heart come evil thoughts and fornications.... They are what pollute you. Mark 7:21-23

Christians are to abstain from fornication.
Acts 15:20, 29

Christians are not to associate with a so-called Christian who commits fornication. 1 Corinthians 5:11

Fornicators shall not inherit the kingdom of God. (Cf. Galatians 5:19-21; Ephesians 5:3-5) 1 Corinthians 6:9

The body was not made for fornication.
1 Corinthians 6:13

Run from sexual immorality; it is a sin against one's own body. 1 Corinthians 6:16, 18

"God wants you to be holy and pure, and to keep clear of all sexual sin." 1 Thessalonians 4:3

The lot of the sexually immoral, fornicators, is the lake that burns with fire and sulphur. (Cf. Revelation 22:15) Revelation 21:8

FREEDOM

"The truth will set you free." John 8:32

"If the Son sets you free, you will indeed be free." John 8:36

"Now you are free from your old master, sin; and you have become slaves to your new master, righteousness." Romans 6:17, 18

Released from the Law. Romans 7:6

Free, in Jesus, from the vicious circle of sin and death. Romans 8:2

A Christian's freedom should not become a stumbling block for someone whose conscience is weak. 1 Corinthians 8:9

A Christian's freedom is not to do wrong but to love and serve one another. (Cf. Galatians 5:1) Galatians 5:13

"Everything God made is good, and we may eat it gladly if we are thankful for it." 1 Timothy 4:4

FRIENDSHIP (Includes Dating)

"How wonderful it is, how pleasant, when brothers live in harmony!" Psalm 133:1

"A true friend is always loyal, and a brother is born to help in time of need." Proverb 17:17

"There are 'friends' who pretend to be friends, but

there is a friend who sticks closer than a brother."
Proverbs 18:24

Two are better than one; if one falls, the other will lift him up. Ecclesiastes 4:9, 10

"How can a Christian be a partner with one who doesn't believe?" 2 Corinthians 6:14, 15

"Enjoy the companionship of those who love the Lord and have pure hearts." 2 Timothy 2:22

If we walk in the light we enjoy fellowship with one another. 1 John 1:7

FRUIT OF THE SPIRIT

Love, Joy, Peace, Patience, Kindness, Goodness, Faithfulness, Gentleness, and Self-control.
Galatians 5:22, 23

GIFTS OF THE SPIRIT

Prophecy, service, teaching, exhorting, giving, leading, showing mercy. Romans 12:6-8

Manifestations of the Holy Spirit.
1 Corinthians 12:7-11

Gifts for service: apostles, prophets, teachers, miracles, healings, helps, administrations, languages.
1 Corinthians 12:28

Prophets, evangelists, pastors and teachers.
Ephesians 4:11

GLUTTONY
See also, Drunkenness

Drunkards and gluttons are on their way to poverty. Proverbs 23:21

Do not make provision to fulfill the lusts of the flesh. Romans 13:14

"Enemies of the cross of Christ...whose god is their appetite." Philippians 3:18, 19

GOSSIP

Do not associate with a gossip. Proverbs 20:19

"Tensions disappear when gossip stops." Proverbs 26:20

Don't speak evil about one another. James 4:11

GRIEF
See also, Depression from rejection, Encouragement, Temptation/Trials

"[God] is a father to the fatherless; he gives justice to the widows." Psalm 68:5

It was good for me that I was afflicted. Psalm 119:71, 75

Even in laughter, the heart may be sad. Proverbs 14:13

So you may not grieve at death as others do who have no hope. 1 Thessalonians 4:13-18

GUIDANCE
See also, Decision-making, Judging

"The Lord will guide you continually, and satisfy you with all good things, and keep you healthy too; and you will be like a well-watered garden, like an everflowing spring." Isaiah 58:11

Divination, astrology, ouija boards, spiritism, are an abomination to God and are forbidden. Deuteronomy 18:10-12

"[God] will teach the ways that are right and best to those who humbly turn to him." Psalm 25:4, 5, 8, 9

"I will instruct you (says the Lord) and guide you along the best pathway for your life." Psalm 32:8

"The steps of good men are directed by the Lord." Psalm 37:5, 23, 24

"God will keep on guiding me all my life." Psalm 73:23, 24

"In everything you do, put God first, and he will direct you." Proverbs 3:5, 6

"Watch your step. Stick to the path and be safe." Proverbs 4:26, 27

"If you leave God's paths and go astray, you will hear a Voice behind you say, 'No, this is the way; walk here.' " Isaiah 30:20, 21

"With good counselors there is safety." (Cf. Proverbs 24:6) Proverbs 11:14

"Plans go wrong with too few counselors; many counselors bring success." (Cf. Proverbs 20:18) Proverbs 15:22

"Since the Lord is directing our steps, why try to understand everything that happens along the way?" Proverbs 20:24

Christians hear Jesus' voice; he knows them; and they follow him. John 10:27

The Holy Spirit shall guide you into all truth. John 16:13

God's gift of the Holy Spirit is for all Christians. Acts 2:38, 39

"All who are led by the Spirit of God are sons of God." Romans 8:14

Pray to have spiritual wisdom and insight and to understand God's will clearly. Colossians 1:9

"If you want to know what God wants you to do, ask him, and he will gladly tell you." James 1:5

GUILT
See Depression

HABIT
See also, Conversion

Old habits are masters we used to serve before God took over our lives. Through Christ, the old gods we worshiped are forgotten ghosts. Isaiah 26:13, 14

A short-tempered man must be rescued again and again. Proverbs 19:19

"Can a leopard take away his spots? Nor can you who are so used to doing evil now start being good."
(Cf. James 3:11, 12) Jeremiah 13:23

A Christian's old self was crucified with Christ so that we should no longer be slaves to sin.
(Cf. Romans 7:18 ff., esp. vv 24, 25)
Romans 6:6, 11-23

HARDNESS
See Love; Pride

HATRED

"Don't hate your brother." Leviticus 19:17

"Hatred stirs old quarrels." Proverbs 10:12

Hate what is evil; cling to what is good. Romans 12:9

"Anyone who hates his Christian brother is really a murderer at heart." 1 John 3:15

HOLINESS
See also, Conduct

Contact with holiness does not necessarily make one holy but contact with the unclean makes one unholy. Haggai 2:12, 13

"Happy are those whose hearts are pure, for they shall see God." Matthew 5:8

Wicked thoughts from a man's heart pollute him.
Mark 7:20-23

Come out and be separate. 2 Corinthians 6:17

"Let us turn away from everything wrong, whether of body or spirit, and purify ourselves." 2 Corinthians 7:1

Bring every thought into subjection to Christ.
2 Corinthians 10:5

"Let heaven fill your thoughts; don't spend your time worrying about things down here." Colossians 3:2

"God has not called us to be dirty-minded and full of lust, but to be holy and clean." 1 Thessalonians 4:7, 8

Dishes of gold and of wood; cleanse yourself to be a dish of purest gold, useful to Christ.
2 Timothy 2:19-21

Jesus gave himself to redeem us from all iniquity and to purify us for himself. Titus 2:14

God's Word judges the thoughts of the heart.
Hebrews 4:12

"One who is not holy will not see the Lord."
Hebrews 12:14

Keep yourself unsoiled by the world. James 1:27

Making friends with the world makes you an enemy of God. James 4:4

"Be holy now in everything you do, just as the Lord is holy." 1 Peter 1:15, 16

"Come away from her, my people; do not take part in her sins, or you will be punished with her."
Revelation 18:4

HOMOSEXUALITY

"Homosexuality is absolutely forbidden, for it is an enormous sin." (Cf. Leviticus 20:13) Leviticus 18:22

"...Men doing shameful things with other men and, as a result, getting paid within their own souls with the penalty they so richly deserved." Romans 1:26, 27, 32

"Homosexuals will have no share in [God's] kingdom.... There was a time when some of you were just like that but now your sins are washed away." (I.e., since the Bible refers to homosexuality as a sin, not a sickness, it is possible to stop.)
1 Corinthians 6:9-11

Sodom and Gomorrah...full of lust of every kind including lust of men for other men; they received the punishment of eternal fire (Cf. Genesis 19:24) Jude 7

HOPE

Do not be afraid, for those with us are more than those against us. 2 Kings 6:16

"The hope of good men is eternal happiness.
Proverbs 10:28

"Hope deferred makes the heart sick." Proverbs 13:12

"You have a wonderful future ahead of you. There is hope for you yet!" Proverbs 23:18

"They that wait upon the Lord shall renew their strength." Isaiah 40:31

"My soul claims the Lord as my inheritance; therefore I will hope in him. The Lord is wonderfully good to those who wait for him." Lamentations 3:24, 25

Through perseverance and the encouragement of the Scriptures we might have hope. Romans 15:4

God granted us his Spirit so we may always be confident that to be away from this body is to be at home with the Lord. 2 Corinthians 5:1-8

"Christ in your hearts is your only hope of glory." Colossians 1:27

Hope in our Lord Jesus Christ. 1 Thessalonians 1:3

"So you will not be full of sorrow, as those are who have no hope." 1 Thessalonians 4:13

HUMILITY

Before honor must come humility. Proverbs 15:33

"'Pride goes before destruction and haughtiness before a fall." Proverbs 16:18

"Better poor and humble than proud and rich." Proverbs 16:19

"True humility and respect for the Lord lead a man to riches, honor and long life." Proverbs 22:4

"Pride ends in a fall, while humility brings honor."
Proverbs 29:23

"Everyone who tries to honor himself shall be humbled; and he who humbles himself shall be honored."
Luke 14:11

"Be honest in your estimate of yourselves."
Romans 12:3

"If a Christian is overcome by some sin, you who are godly should gently and humbly help him back onto the right path, remembering that next time it might be one of you who is in the wrong." Galatians 6:1

"Be humble, thinking of others as better than yourself."
Philippians 2:3

"God gives strength to the humble, but sets himself against the proud and haughty." (Cf. Psalm 138:6; 1 Peter 5:5) James 4:6

"If you will humble yourselves under the mighty hand of God, in his good time he will lift you up."
(Cf. James 4:10) 1 Peter 5:6

INSECURITY
See Security

JEALOUSLY
See also, Envy

Jealousy enrages a man. Proverbs 6:34, NASB

"Jealousy is more dangerous and cruel than anger."
Proverbs 27:4

Put off jealousy. Romans 13:13

Jealousy is not desirable. 2 Corinthians 12:20

Jealousy is a deed of the flesh, opposed to the fruit of the Spirit. (Cf. 1 Corinthians 3:3) Galatians 5:19, 20

"Wherever there is jealousy or selfish ambition, there will be disorder and every other kind of evil."
James 3:14-16

JUDGING (by man)

"Don't criticize, and then you won't be criticized."
(Cf. Luke 6:37-42) Matthew 7:1-5

Stop judging by appearances and make a righteous judgment. John 7:24

A wise person, able to decide between Christians.
1 Corinthians 6:5

Let two or three prophets speak and the others judge.
1 Corinthians 14:29

Let no one judge you regarding food and drink, festivals, sabbaths. Colossians 2:16

"Do not scoff at those who prophesy, but test everything that is said to be sure it is true, and if it is, then accept it." 1 Thessalonians 5:20, 21

"Learn right from wrong by practicing doing right."
Hebrews 5:14

It is a sin to show partiality. James 2:1-9

"What right do you have to judge or criticize others?" James 4:11, 12

"Don't always believe everything you hear just because someone says it is a message from God: test it first to see if it really is." 1 John 4:1

JUDGMENT (of man)

"God will judge us for everything we do, including every hidden thing, good or bad." Ecclesiastes 12:14

Every idle word will be accounted for. Matthew 12:36

Wicked people will be cast into the fire; there will be weeping and gnashing of teeth. Matthew 13:40-50

"All that is now hidden will someday come to light." (Cf. Luke 12:2, 3) Mark 4:22

He who believes in Jesus is not judged but he who doesn't believe is already judged. John 3:18

"Each of us will stand personally before the Judgment Seat of God." Romans 14:10-12

"Everyone's work will be put through the fire." 1 Corinthians 3:13

"We must all stand before Christ to be judged....Each of us will receive whatever he deserves for the good or bad things he has done." 2 Corinthians 5:10

Jesus will appear, "bringing judgment on those who...refuse to accept his plan to save them." (Cf. Ephesians 5:6) 2 Thessalonians 1:7-9

"Everything about us is bare and wide open to the all-seeing eyes of our living God; nothing can be hidden from him." Hebrews 4:13

"It is destined that men die only once, and after that comes judgment." Hebrews 9:27

"If anyone sins deliberately by rejecting the Savior after knowing the truth of forgiveness... there will be nothing to look forward to but the terrible punishment of God's awful anger." Hebrews 10:26, 27

" 'Justice belongs to me; I will repay them.... It is a fearful thing to fall into the hands of the living God." Hebrews 10:30, 31

Teachers will incur a greater judgment. James 3:1

Punishment of false teachers. 2 Peter 2:1-8

Great White Throne Judgment. Revelation 20:11-15

LAZINESS
See also, Work

"Take a lesson from the ants, you lazy fellow." Proverbs 6:6-11

"Lazy people want much but get little, while the diligent are prospering." Proverbs 13:4

LONELINESS

"The Lord is my Shepherd.... You are close beside me." Psalm 23

"Fear not, for I am with you. Do not be dismayed. I am your God." Isaiah 41:10

"When you go through deep waters and great trouble, I will be with you." Isaiah 43:2

Jesus: "I am with you always, even to the end of the world." Matthew 28:20

"God has said, 'I will never, *never* fail you nor forsake you.'" Hebrews 13:5

LOVE

There are several words in the original Greek language of the New Testament which are translated by the English word, *love*. Of the three most common, *eros*, meaning a sensual, erotic love, is not found in the Bible. The other two are *agape* and *philia*. *Philia* is an emotional love—a good, pleasant feeling about someone or something. *Philia* is sometimes combined with the word for brother, *adelphos*, into *philadelphia*. This word refers to the warm, common affection, love, that one has toward Christian brothers and sisters. *Agape* is not an emotional love; it gets started in the mind as a conscious act of will. *Agape* means to hold in high regard, to appreciate the worth of, and then to act upon that regard. There may or may not be some action resulting from *philia* but *agape*, by definition, results in some action.

In the following list, *agape*-love is indicated by (A) and *philia*-love and its verb form, *phileo*, and its combining form, *philadelphia*, by (P).

"Love overlooks insults." Proverbs 10:12

"Love (A) your enemies!" Matthew 5:44

"Love (A) [the Lord God] with all your heart and soul and mind and strength. Love (A) others as much as yourself." Mark 12:30, 31

See:
"Loving (A) God means doing what he tells us to do."
1 John 5:3

"God loved (A) the world so much that he gave his only Son so that anyone who believes in him shall not perish but have eternal life." John 3:16

Compare:
"We know what real love (A) is from Christ's example in dying for us. And so we also ought to lay down our lives for our Christian brothers." 1 John 3:16

He that loves (P) his life will lose it. John 12:25

Love (A) one another. (Cf. John 15:12, 17)
John 13:34, 35

The Father loves (P) the person who loves (P) Jesus.
John 16:27

"Love (P) each other with brotherly affection."
Romans 12:10

Love (A) does no wrong to anyone and so fulfills the Law. Romans 13:10

"Love (A) is very patient and kind, never jealous or envious, never boastful or proud, never haughty or selfish or rude. Love does not demand its own way. It is not irritable or touchy. It does not hold grudges and will hardly even notice when others do it wrong. It is never glad about injustice, but rejoices whenever truth wins out. If you love someone you will be loyal to him no matter what the cost. You will always believe in him, always expect the best of him, and always stand your ground in defending him." 1 Corinthians 13:4-7

The love (A) of Christ that "is so great that you will

never see the end of it or fully know or understand it."
Ephesians 3:19

"Be full of love (A) for others, following the example of Christ, who loved you and gave himself to God as a sacrifice to take away your sins." Ephesians 5:2

Older women should train younger women to be loving (P) wives and mothers. Titus 2:3, 4

"Continue to love (P) each other." Hebrews 13:1

"Now you can have real love (P) for everyone because your souls have been cleansed from selfishness and hatred when you trusted Christ to save you; so see to it that you really do love (A) each other warmly."
1 Peter 1:22

Love (A) one another...for God is love (A).
1 John 4:7, 8

Love (A) expels fear. 1 John 4:18

NOTE: *All* occurrences of the word *love* in the entire book of 1 John are translations of the Greek word *agape* or its verb form, *agapao*.

LUST
See Desire

LYING

The ninth commandment is, "You must not lie."
Exodus 20:16

God will destroy those who lie. Psalm 5:6

Concealing hatred is lying. Proverbs 10:18

Lying is an abomination to God. Proverbs 12:22

The devil is the father of lies. John 8:44

"Stop lying to each other; tell the truth."
Ephesians 4:25

"Don't tell lies to each other." Colossians 3:9

NARCOTICS
See Drugs

NERVOUSNESS
See Fear

OBEDIENCE
See also, Authority

"Obedience is far better than sacrifice" (i.e., better than religious ritual). 1 Samuel 15:22

The prophet believed a lying prophet and disobeyed God—and was killed. 1 Kings 13:11-32

The willing and obedient will eat of the fruit of the land. Isaiah 1:19, 20

The Rechabites were honored because they would not disobey God and their father by drinking wine even though it was offered to them by a prophet.
Jeremiah 35:1-19

When told to do something which would require disobeying God, offer a constructive alternative. Daniel 1:8-16

Not everyone who calls Jesus "Lord," will enter heaven, but only those who obey God. Matthew 7:21

He who obeys Jesus will remain in his love. John 15:10

"We must obey God rather than men." Acts 5:29

"The Holy Spirit...is given by God to all who obey him." Acts 5:32

Children, obey your parents that it may be well with you. (Cf. Colossians 3:20) Ephesians 6:1-3

Jesus learned obedience. Hebrews 5:8

OCCULT

There are eight practices which are offensive and an abomination to God. (Deuteronomy 18:10-12—Cf. Leviticus 19:26-31; 20:27; and, esp., 20:6):
1. Divination (fortune-telling, palm reading, water-witching, etc.)
2. Witchcraft/soothsaying (i.e., an observer of times; astrology)
3. Observing/interpreting omens (witchcraft)
4. Sorcery (use of drugs)
5. Charming; one who casts a spell or hex (hypnotism; witchcraft)
6. Contacting the spirit world (a medium)
7. Spiritism; a wizard (all occult practices including ouija boards)
8. Calling up the dead; a necromancer

"Can the living find out the future from the dead?"
Isaiah 8:19

We are fighting against the spiritual forces of evil—use the armor of God. Ephesians 6:10-18

"Give yourselves humbly to God. Resist the devil and he will flee from you." James 4:7, 8

"There is someone in your hearts who is stronger than any evil teacher in this wicked world." 1 John 4:4

PEACE

"When a man is trying to please God, God makes even his worst enemies to be at peace with him."
Proverbs 16:7

Jesus said, "My peace I give to you." John 14:27

"I have told you all this so that you will have peace of heart and mind. Here on earth you will have many trials and sorrows; but cheer up, for I have overcome the world." John 16:33

"Be at peace with everyone, just as much as possible." Romans 12:18

Aim for one another's peace and development.
Romans 14:19

"God's peace, which is far more wonderful than the human mind can understand."
Philippians 4:6, 7

Let the peace of Christ arbitrate (act as referee) in your heart. Colossians 3:15

Seek for peace with everyone. Hebrews 12:14

PRAYER

God will not listen if we cherish sin in our heart.
Psalm 66:17, 18

God gave the Israelites what they prayed for, but he sent leanness in their souls. Psalm 106:15

"Let me see your kindness to me in the morning...for my prayer is sincere." Psalm 143:8

"God doesn't listen to the prayers of men who flout the law." Proverbs 28:9

When you make a vow to God, be sure to pay it—it is better to not vow than to vow and not pay it.
Ecclesiastes 5:4, 5

Sin separates one from God and he hides his face so that he can not hear. Isaiah 59:1, 2

O great and mighty God:...nothing is too hard for you. Jeremiah 32:17-19

Let us search and try our ways. Lamentations 3:40, 41

"I called upon your name, O Lord...and you heard me!" Lamentations 3:55, 56

"No one can get to the Father except by means of me." (Jesus) John 14:6

Husbands: treat your wife as you should so that your prayers will not be hindered. 1 Peter 3:7

The Lord is attentive to the prayers of the righteous.
1 Peter 3:12

If those who believe in Jesus ask in agreement with God's will, he hears and will answer. 1 John 5:13-15

PRIDE

"Proud men end in shame." Proverbs 11:2

"A fool thinks he needs no advice, but a wise man listens to others." (Cf. Proverbs 14:12) Proverbs 12:15

"Pride leads to arguments." Proverbs 13:10

"Pride goes before destruction." Proverbs 16:18

"Pride ends in a fall." Proverbs 29:23

Let him who boasts boast that he understands and knows God. Jeremiah 9:24

"Your heart was filled with pride." Ezekiel 28:13-17

We may take pride in behavior with godly sincerity and holiness. It is ours by divine grace, not by our own skills. 2 Corinthians 1:12

"If anyone is going to boast, let him boast about what the Lord has done and not about himself."
2 Corinthians 10:17, 18

PURITY
See Holiness

REBELLION
See Obedience

RECONCILIATION
See also, Repentance

Leave the altar and be reconciled with your brother. Matthew 5:23, 24

If your brother wrongs you. Matthew 18:15-17

If your brother sins and repents. Luke 17:3, 4

REJECTION
See Depression

REPENTANCE (involving restitution when appropriate)
See also, Depression, Reconciliation

"A broken and a contrite heart, O God, you will not ignore." Psalm 51:17

"Prove by the way you live that you really have repented." Luke 3:8

"You, too, will perish unless you repent." Luke 13:3, 5

If your brother sins, rebuke him, and if he repents, forgive him. Luke 17:3, 4

"Forgiveness of sins for all who turn to [Jesus]." Luke 24:47

Repent and turn to God so that your sins may be wiped away. (Cf. Acts 2:38, 39) Acts 3:19

God overlooked times of ignorance but now is calling people to repentance. Acts 17:30

"All must forsake their sins and turn to God—and prove their repentance by doing good deeds."
Acts 26:20

"[God's] kindness is meant to lead you to repentance."
Romans 2:4

Godly sorrow brings repentance that leads to salvation.
2 Corinthians 7:10

It is impossible for those once enlightened, if they fall away, to be brought back to repentance.
Hebrews 6:4-8

"[God] is not willing that any should perish, and he is giving more time for sinners to repent." 2 Peter 3:9

Repent and do the things you did at first (i.e., your first love of Christ). Revelation 2:4, 5

Those whom God loves he rebukes and disciplines, so be earnest and repent. Revelation 3:19

REPROVE
See also, Discipline

"Don't hate your brother. Rebuke anyone who sins; don't let him get away with it, or you will be equally guilty." Leviticus 19:17

A mocker will hate you for rebuking him but a wise man will love you all the more. Proverbs 9:8

"If you refuse to discipline your son, it proves you don't love him." Proverbs 13:24

"A youngster's heart is filled with rebellion, but punishment will drive it out of him." Proverbs 22:15

"Don't fail to correct your children."
(Cf. Proverbs 19:18) Proverbs 23:13, 14

"In the end, people appreciate frankness more than flattery." Proverbs 28:23

"Scolding and spanking a child helps him to learn. Left to himself, he brings shame to his mother."
Proverbs 29:15

"Discipline your son and he will give you happiness and peace of mind." Proverbs 29:17

When sinners are not quickly punished, people think it is safe to do wrong. Ecclesiastes 8:11

If you warn a wicked man and he doesn't change, he will die but you are blameless—you have done all you could. Ezekiel 3:19

If you don't warn a wicked man, God will hold you responsible. Ezekiel 33:8, 9

"Rebuke your brother if he sins." Luke 17:3

"If he has really sinned, then he should be rebuked in front of the whole church so that no one else will follow his example." 1 Timothy 5:20

If someone strays from the truth, the one who brings him back will save his soul. James 5:19, 20

RESENTMENT
See also, Bitterness, Forgiveness

"A man with hate in his heart may sound pleasant enough, but don't believe him; for he is cursing you in his heart. Though he pretends to be so kind, his hatred will finally come to light for all to see."
Proverbs 26:24-26

REVENGE
See Forgiveness

SALVATION (need)

"Consider your ways: You plant much but harvest little. You have scarcely enough to eat or drink, and not enough clothes to keep you warm. Your income disappears, as though you were putting it into pockets filled with holes! 'Think it over,' says the Lord of Hosts."
Haggai 1:6, 7

"How long are you going to waver between two opinions? If the Lord is God, *follow* Him!" 1 Kings 18:21

What hope has the godless when he dies? Will God hear his cry? (No) Job 27:8, 9

No one remembers God when he is dead—it is too late to praise him from the grave. Psalm 6:5

Pray to God while he may be found. Psalm 32:6

"Seek the Lord while you can find him." Isaiah 55:6

All our righteous acts are like filthy rags. Isaiah 64:6

The one who sins shall die. Ezekiel 18:4, 20

"If a wicked person turns away from all his sins...he shall surely live." Ezekiel 18:21

A good man who turns from being good and begins sinning shall die for the evil he has done. Ezekiel 18:26

God wants the sinner to turn and live; he takes no pleasure in the death of anyone. Ezekiel 18:23, 32

God's eyes are too pure to look on evil. Habakkuk 1:13

God said, "I called but they refused to listen, so when they cried to me, I turned away." Zechariah 7:13

"How does a man benefit if he gains the whole world and loses his soul in the process?" Mark 8:36

"Real life and real living are not related to how rich we are." Luke 12:15

"Fool! Tonight you die. Then who will get it all?" Luke 12:16-20

It is God's will that everyone believe in Jesus and have eternal life. John 6:40

"Right now God is ready to welcome you. Today he is ready to save you." 2 Corinthians 6:2

"The Holy Spirit warns us to listen to him, to be careful to hear his voice today and not let our hearts become set against him." Hebrews 3:7-11

"Men die only once, and after that comes judgment." Hebrews 9:27

God doesn't want for any to perish but for all to repent. 2 Peter 3:9

SALVATION (means)
See also, Repentance

You will seek Me and find Me, when you search for Me with all your heart. Jeremiah 29:13, NASB

The Son was named Jesus because he would save his people from their sins. Matthew 1:21

Jesus is our rest; his burden is light. Matthew 11:28-30

Repentance leads to forgiveness of sins. Luke 24:47

Those who receive Jesus have the right to become children of God. John 1:12

You must be born again. John 3:3-8

"God loved the world so much that he gave his only Son so that anyone who believes in him shall not perish but have eternal life." John 3:16

"All who trust him—God's Son—to save them have eternal life; those who don't believe and obey him shall never see heaven, but the wrath of God remains upon them." John 3:36

Jesus will not reject any who come to him. John 6:37

Jesus gives his sheep eternal life and no one will snatch them away from him. John 10:27, 28

Jesus is the Way, the Truth, and the Life; no one can get to the Father except through him. John 14:6

There is salvation in no one else except Jesus. Acts 4:12

There is no condemnation for those who are in Christ

Jesus...who do not live according to their sinful nature but according to the Spirit. Romans 8:1, 4

"The Holy Spirit speaks to us deep in our hearts, and tells us that we really are God's children."
Romans 8:16

"Nothing will ever be able to separate us from the love of God demonstrated by our Lord Jesus Christ when he died for us." Romans 8:38, 39

"If you tell others with your own mouth that Jesus Christ is your Lord, and believe in your own heart that God has raised him from the dead, you will be saved." Romans 10:9

Christ died for our sins; he rose from the dead and was seen by many. 1 Corinthians 15:3-6

Christ died for all that we might live for him.
2 Corinthians 5:15

Jesus was made sin on our behalf. 2 Corinthians 5:21

"God sometimes uses sorrow in our lives to help us turn away from sin and seek eternal life."
2 Corinthians 7:10

We are saved by grace, through faith, for good works.
Ephesians 2:8-10

He saved us through the washing of regeneration and a renewing by the Holy Spirit. Titus 3:4-7

We are made to share in Christ if we hold firmly till the end the confidence we had at first. Hebrews 3:14

The righteous shall live by faith but God is not pleased with one who shrinks back. Hebrews 10:38, 39

"Anyone who wants to come to God must believe that there is a God and that he rewards those who sincerely look for him." Hebrews 11:6

Eternal life is in God's Son; he who has the Son has that life; he who does not have the Son does not have life. 1 John 5:11-13

SCRIPTURE

"Open my eyes to see wonderful things in your Word." Psalm 119:18

"God's laws are pure, eternal, just. They are more desirable than gold." Psalm 19:7-11

"How can a young man stay pure? By reading your Word and following its rules." Psalm 119:9-11

God's Word gives light and understanding to the simple. Psalm 119:130

God has exalted his Word above all things. Psalm 138:2

"Every word of God proves true.... Do not add to his words." Proverbs 30:5, 6

"Search the Book of the Lord and see all that he will do." Isaiah 34:16

"The grass withers, the flowers fade, but the Word of our God shall stand forever." (Cf. 1 Peter 1:25; Psalm 119:89) Isaiah 40:8

God's Word will always accomplish all he wants it to. Isaiah 55:11

If anyone really wants to do God's will he will understand Jesus' teaching. John 7:17

If you live in God's Word (live as he tells you to), you will know the truth and the truth will set you free. John 8:31, 32

God's Word is truth. John 17:17

Through patience and the encouragement of Scripture we might have hope. Romans 15:4

The Word of God is the sword of the Spirit. Ephesians 6:17

Present yourself approved to God, correctly handling his Word. 2 Timothy 2:15

Scripture is God-breathed and is useful for teaching, rebuking, correcting, and training in righteousness. 2 Timothy 3:16

Scripture equips the man of God adequately for all good works. 2 Timothy 3:17

The Word of God is living and active. Hebrews 4:12

Scripture is not self-explanatory (able to be understood by mental effort—Cf. 1 Corinthians 2:14: spiritual things are spiritually understood). 2 Peter 1:20

No prophecy of Scripture came from man but from the Holy Spirit. 2 Peter 1:21

Do not go beyond what is written (in Scripture). Revelation 22:18

SECURITY

"Who then can ever keep Christ's love from us? When we have trouble or calamity, when we are hunted down or destroyed, is it because he doesn't love us anymore? And if we are hungry, or penniless, or in danger, or threatened with death, has God deserted us? No,...For I am convinced that nothing can ever separate us from his love. Death can't, and life can't. The angels won't, and all the powers of hell itself cannot keep God's love away. Our fears for today, our worries about tomorrow, or where we are—high above the sky, or in the deepest ocean—nothing will ever be able to separate us from the love of God demonstrated by our Lord Jesus Christ when he died for us." Romans 8:35-39

"It is better to trust the Lord than to put confidence in men." Psalm 118:8

"All who listen to [God] shall live in peace and safety, unafraid." Proverbs 1:33

SELF-WILL
See Authority

SEX / SEXUALITY
See also, Adultery, Fornication

"Although the man and his wife were both naked, neither of them was embarrassed or ashamed." Genesis 2:25

"If a man joins himself to a prostitute she becomes a part of him and he becomes a part of her." 1 Corinthians 6:16

Husbands and wives are to fulfill their marital duties to each other. 1 Corinthians 7:3-5

"Deaden the evil desires lurking within you; have nothing to do with sexual sin, impurity, lust and shameful desires." Colossians 3:5

"Keep clear of all sexual sin so that each of you will marry in holiness and honor—not in lustful passion as the heathen do, in their ignorance of God."
1 Thessalonians 4:3-5

Women are not to dominate men. 1 Timothy 2:11-15

No longer live by human desires but for what God wants. 1 Peter 4:2, 3

SHAME

"Proud men end in shame, but the meek become wise." Proverbs 11:2

"If you refuse criticism you will end in poverty and disgrace; if you accept criticism you are on the road to fame." Proverbs 13:18

Maintain a clear conscience so you won't be shamed.
1 Peter 3:16

SIN

The country shall be completely emptied and utterly looted; for the Lord has spoken the word. The earth mourns and fades away; the world languishes and withers; the most prominent of the people shall

languish. The land lies polluted by its inhabitants, because they have transgressed the Law, violated the statutes, and broken the everlasting covenant. Therefore a curse is consuming the land, and the people living in it are found guilty; therefore the inhabitants of the earth are scorched, and few men are left.
Isaiah 24:3-6

Even from birth the wicked go astray and speak lies.
Psalm 58:3

"All have sinned; all fall short of God's glorious ideal."
Romans 3:23

"The wages of sin is death." Romans 6:23

Everything that does not come from faith is sin.
Romans 14:23

"Knowing what is right to do and then not doing it is sin." James 4:17

Whoever practices sin has not really known Jesus.
1 John 3:6

STEALING

The eighth commandment is, "You must not steal."
Exodus 20:15

Regarding stealing food when starving.
Proverbs 6:30, 31

"The Lord despises every kind of cheating."
Proverbs 20:10

"A man who assists a thief must really hate himself!"
Proverbs 29:24

The thief must steal no more, but work.
Ephesians 4:28

SUICIDE
See Encouragement

TALK
See also, Gossip, Lying

"Don't make any vows!... Your word is enough."
(Cf. James 5:12) Matthew 5:34-37

Every idle word will be accounted for. Matthew 12:36

There should be no obscenity, foolish talk, or coarse joking. Ephesians 5:3, 4

It is shameful to even mention the secret deeds done in darkness. Ephesians 5:12

"Don't criticize and speak evil about each other."
(Cf. James 5:9) James 4:11

Do not say, "We shall do this," but, "If the Lord wills, we shall do this." James 4:13-16

"If you want a happy, good life, keep control of your tongue, and guard your lips from telling lies."
(Cf. Psalm 34:12, 13) 1 Peter 3:10

TEMPTATION / TRIALS

"God left [Hezekiah] to himself in order to test him and to see what he was really like." 2 Chronicles 32:31

If sinners entice you, don't consent. Proverbs 1:10

"Silver and gold are purified by fire, but God purifies hearts." Proverbs 17:3

God is able to save; yet, even if he doesn't, trust him; walk with the Son of God. Daniel 3:16-25

"I have told you all this so that you will have peace of heart and mind. Here on earth you will have many trials and sorrows; but cheer up, for I have overcome the world." John 16:33

Trials bring perseverance, which brings proven character, which brings hope. Romans 5:3, 4

No temptation will befall you except what other people experience. 1 Corinthians 10:13

God comforts us in our troubles so we can encourage others in theirs. 2 Corinthians 1:3, 4

Though our bodies are dying, our inner person is renewed; momentary distress produces God's richest blessings for us. 2 Corinthians 4:16, 17

Everyone who wants to live a godly life in Christ Jesus will be persecuted. 2 Timothy 3:12

"Since [Jesus] himself has now been through suffering and temptation, he knows what it is like when we suffer and are tempted, and he is wonderfully able to help us." Hebrews 2:18

Jesus, "understands our weaknesses, since he had the same temptations we do, though he never once gave way to them and sinned." Hebrews 4:15

Be happy when trials are encountered because testing produces patience and makes us complete. James 1:2-4

God cannot be tempted by evil and he tempts no one. James 1:13

"Temptation is the pull of man's own evil thoughts and wishes." James 1:14, 15

Trials test your faith as fire tests gold and purifies it. 1 Peter 1:6, 7

It is commendable if a man bears up under the pain of unjust suffering. 1 Peter 2:19

"Don't be bewildered or surprised when you go through the fiery trials ahead, for this is no strange, unusual thing that is going to happen to you.... So if you are suffering according to God's will, keep on doing what is right and trust yourself to the God who made you, for he will never fail you." 1 Peter 4:12, 19

THINKING / THOUGHTS

"It is the thought-life that pollutes...All these vile things come from within." Mark 7:20-23

Bring every thought into subjection to Christ. 2 Corinthians 10:5

Let your mind dwell on whatever is true, noble, right, pure, lovely, admirable, excellent, praiseworthy. Philippians 4:8

Let no one take you captive through hollow and deceitful, worldly philosophy based on human traditions. Colossians 2:8

"Let heaven fill your thoughts; don't spend your time worrying about things down here." Colossians 3:2

The Word of God judges the thoughts of the heart. Hebrews 4:12

UNFORGIVENESS
See Forgiveness

WORK

God put man in the garden to cultivate it. Genesis 2:15

The soil is cursed; by toil and sweat, man must make a living. Genesis 3:17-19

"Unless the Lord builds a house, the builders' work is useless." Psalm 127:1

"The Lord's blessing is our greatest wealth. All our work adds nothing to it." Proverbs 10:22

"Work brings profit; talk brings poverty!" Proverbs 14:23

"Commit your work to the Lord, then it will succeed." Proverbs 16:3

"A lazy man is brother to the saboteur." Proverbs 18:9

"Don't weary yourself trying to get rich." Proverbs 23:4

Description of a godly woman's work. Proverbs 31:10-31

"The man who works hard sleeps well."
Ecclesiastes 5:12

Give yourself fully to the work of the Lord, because labor in the Lord is not in vain. 1 Corinthians 15:58

"Work hard and cheerfully at all you do, just as though you were working for the Lord." Colossians 3:23, 24

"Stay away from any Christian who spends his days in laziness.... He who does not work shall not eat."
2 Thessalonians 3:6-15

WORRY

Be still (without care) and know that I am God.
Psalm 46:10

"We live within the shadow of the Almighty, sheltered by the God who is above all gods... he alone is my refuge." Psalm 91

"Anxious hearts are very heavy." Proverbs 12:25

"A relaxed attitude lengthens a man's life.
Proverbs 14:30

"A cheerful heart does good like medicine."
Proverbs 17:22

"Don't worry about *things*... don't be anxious about tomorrow." (Cf. Luke 12:22-31) Matthew 6:25-34

Don't worry; tell God your needs; his peace will guard your hearts. Philippians 4:6, 7

"Let [God] have all your worries and cares, for he is always thinking about you and watching everything that concerns you." (Cf. Psalm 55:22) 1 Peter 5:7

SECTION II
Counseling Aids

ATTITUDE DEVELOPMENT CHART

To aid those who counsel only occasionally, we include here a graphic presentation of attitude development. This diagram shows development patterns and depicts how many problem areas develop from six root causes. It is greatly simplified and, therefore, can only be used as a guide when clues to a counselee's problem are minimal. Caution: it does not have universal application but only when the root causes are internal and not external.

One way this diagram might be used is with a counselee who has a presentation problem of drunkenness. A quick glance at the diagram indicates that this possibly stems from lust, which, in turn, stems from covetousness. In listening to the counselee, the counselor is thus alerted to pay particular attention to statements related to these areas.

Each directional arrow between major attitude areas is numbered. The accompanying list of symptoms is cross-referenced to these lines. Sometimes the counselor is able to notice a symptom, for example, of lethargy—the counselee completely lacks motivation. By using the diagram, it can be seen that a common cause of lethargy is bitterness and, again, the counselor is alerted to what to listen for.

In either case, the object is to be able to apply appropriate scriptural guidance to the situation as quickly as possible.

THE PATH OF ATTITUDE DEVELOPMENT

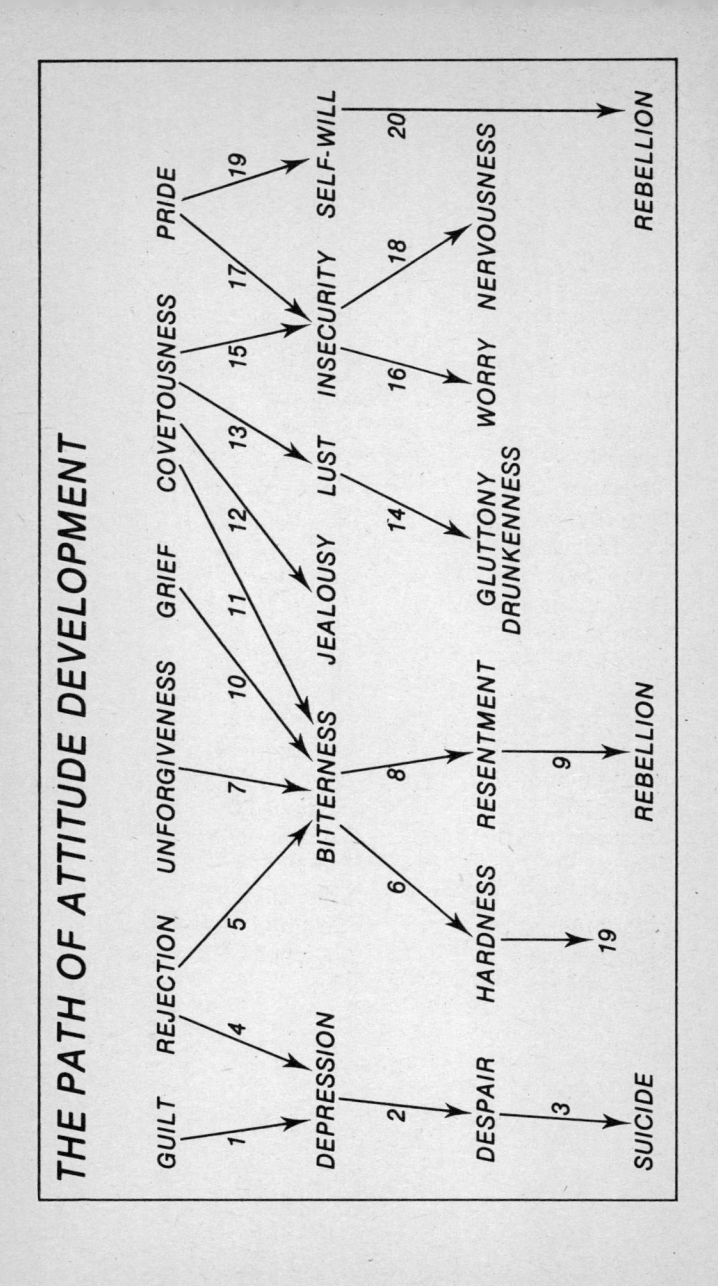

GUILT —1→ DEPRESSION —2→ DESPAIR —3→ SUICIDE

REJECTION —4→ DEPRESSION

REJECTION —5→ BITTERNESS

BITTERNESS —6→ HARDNESS —19→

BITTERNESS —8→ RESENTMENT —9→ REBELLION

UNFORGIVENESS —7→ BITTERNESS

GRIEF —10→ BITTERNESS

COVETOUSNESS —11→ BITTERNESS

COVETOUSNESS —12→ JEALOUSY

COVETOUSNESS —13→ LUST

LUST —14→ GLUTTONY / DRUNKENNESS

COVETOUSNESS —15→ INSECURITY

INSECURITY —16→ WORRY / NERVOUSNESS

PRIDE —17→ INSECURITY

INSECURITY —18→

PRIDE —19→ SELF-WILL —20→ REBELLION

SYMPTOMS RELATED TO MAJOR ATTITUDES

Alcohol 3
Anger 19
Anxiety 16
Combativeness 8
Compulsive eating 14
Condemnation 1
Criticism 17
Cruelty 6, 8
Crying 16
Daydreaming 13
Defeatism 3
Dejection 2
Despondency 3
Destructiveness 6
Discouragement 2
Disobedience 19
Distrust 15
Dread 16
Drugs 3
Envy 13
Fantasizing 13
Fault-finding 17
Fear 16
Frustration 14
Gloom 2
Hatred 8, 9
Heartbreak 10
Hopelessness 3
Hurt 6

Idleness 6, 8
Inadequacy 18
Indifference 6
Inferiority 16
Insomnia 16
Lethargy 6
Listlessness 6
Loneliness 18
Murder 20
Passivity 6
Pouting 19
Restlessness 18
Sadism 8
Sadness 10
Selfishness 19
Self-pity 16
Shame 1
Shyness 18
Spite 8
Stoicism 6
Stubborness 20
Suspicion 15
Temper 17
Tension 18
Timidity 18
Unreality 13
Unsubmissiveness 20
Violence 20

COUNSELING CHECK LIST

As a further aid to those not professionally trained in counseling we offer the following check list of things which should characterize every counseling session:

1. Determine whether evangelism is indicated. If the counselee is not a Christian, salvation is the most important goal. God's promises are conditional and one major condition is usually salvation.

2. Determine if a medical check-up would be advisable. Be alert to possible physical causes of abnormal behavior. For example, significant sleep loss can cause effects similar to LSD use. Also, recent discoveries indicate that abnormal behavior, from depression to schizophrenia, may be caused by diet-related problems, either poor nutrition or allergic reaction to food additives.

Investigation has revealed that all of the following symptoms and more may be related to hypoglycemia—low blood sugar:

nervousness
exhaustion
irritability
depression
drowsiness
unprovoked anxiety
phobias
nightmares

nervous breakdown
mental confusion
lack of concentration
unsocial or antisocial behavior

Especially in cases of chronic occurrences of these and other abnormal behavior patterns, it would never be out of line to recommend, even insist, on a check-up by a physician, especially one knowledgeable in nutrition, and to suggest a five- or six-hour glucose tolerance test.

3. Check on homework from the previous session. If undone, do not continue but postpone the session until homework is finished. (See item 11.)

4. Sort out responsibilities: among the counselees or between the counselee and others who may be involved.

5. Gather concrete data. Stress *what* rather than *why*.

6. Distinguish and separate:
   a. The Presentation Problem: what he *says* is wrong.
   b. The Performance Problem: what he did that he shouldn't have done or didn't do that he should have—usually presented as an *effect* when it's really a *cause*.
   c. The Preconditioning Problem: the underlying habitual response pattern of which the performance problem is but one instance.

7. Talk not only about the problems—talk also about God's solutions.

8. Check motivation. Ultimately, the only valid

motivation for doing what God says is loving obedience: because God says so.

9. Insist on obedience to God regardless of feelings or modern humanistic ethics.

10. Check all items written as notes during interview with counselee.

11. Give concrete homework at every session. When necessary, explain how to do it. Begin with single-stranded, simple problems and tasks.